# BEAVERS
## IN AMERICAN HISTORY

NORMAN D. GRAUBART

**PowerKiDS** press
New York

Published in 2015 by The Rosen Publishing Group, Inc.
29 East 21st Street, New York, NY 10010

First Edition

Editor: Amelie von Zumbusch
Photo Research: Katie Stryker
Book Design: Colleen Bialecki

Photo Credits: Cover Stock Montage/Contributor/Archive Photos/Getty Images; p. 4 studioworxx/iStock/Thinkstock; pp. 5, 19 Alfred Jacob Miller/The Walters Art Museum; p. 6 Brian Lasenby/Shutterstock.com; p. 8 Civdis/Shutterstock.com; p. 9 (top) hubert/Shutterstock.com; p. 9 (bottom) Steve Raubenstine/iStock/Thinkstock; p. 10 Marilyn Angel Wynn/Nativestock/Getty Images; p. 11 Steve Estvanik/iStock/Thinkstock; p. 12 Encyclopaedia Britannica/Contributor/Universal Images Group/Getty Images; p. 13 (top) Photo Researchers/Getty Images; p. 13 (bottom) Underwood Archives/Contributor/Archive Photos/Getty Images; p. 15 British Library/Robana/Contributor/Hulton Fine Art Collection/Getty Images; p. 16 Ekspansio/iStock/Thinkstock; p. 17 MPI/Stringer/Archive Photos/Getty Images; p. 18 Stock Montage/Contributor/Archive Photos/Getty Images; p. 21 Alan Jeffery/Shutterstock.com; p. 22 Simon Phipps/iStock/Thinkstock.

Library of Congress Cataloging-in-Publication Data

Graubart, Norman D.
Beavers in American history / by Norman D. Graubart. — First edition.
    pages cm. — (How animals shaped history)
Includes index.
ISBN 978-1-4777-6753-5 (library binding) — ISBN 978-1-4777-6754-2 (pbk.) — ISBN 978-1-4777-6625-5 (6-pack)
1. American beaver—History—United States—Juvenile literature. 2. Fur trade—United States—History—Juvenile literature. I. Title.
QL737.R632G73 2015
599.37—dc23

                                    2013046671

Manufactured in the United States of America

CPSIA Compliance Information: Batch # W14PK5: For Further Information contact Rosen Publishing, New York, New York at 1-800-237-9932

# CONTENTS

Have you ever seen a beaver in the wild or in a zoo? Beavers are **mammals** that make their homes along the banks of rivers and streams. They are members of the rodent family. This means they are related to rabbits, rats, and mice.

There are two species, or kinds, of beavers. North American beavers, such as this one, live in North America. Eurasian beavers live in Europe and Asia.

4

Alfred Jacob Miller made this painting of trappers setting out to hunt beavers between 1858 and 1860. It was based on drawings he had made in 1838 when he visited what is now Wyoming.

People have been trapping beavers for centuries to use their fur for coats, blankets, and hats. Just as Europeans began to explore North America in the 1600s, the beaver **population** in Europe was dying out. The Europeans traded with Native Americans for North American beaver skins. This fur trade grew quickly and played a big part in the early American **economy**.

Beavers have three features that make them easy to spot. First, they have four strong front teeth. These teeth can cut through wood easily. Second, beavers have large, flat tails. They use their tails to steer themselves while swimming. Finally, beavers have thick, brown fur. Historically, humans mostly found beavers useful for their fur. People also trapped beavers to make perfume out of a substance that beavers make called castoreum.

Beavers eat the inner bark, leaves, and twigs of trees, such as willows, aspens, birches, cottonwoods, and maples. They also eat the roots and buds of water plants.

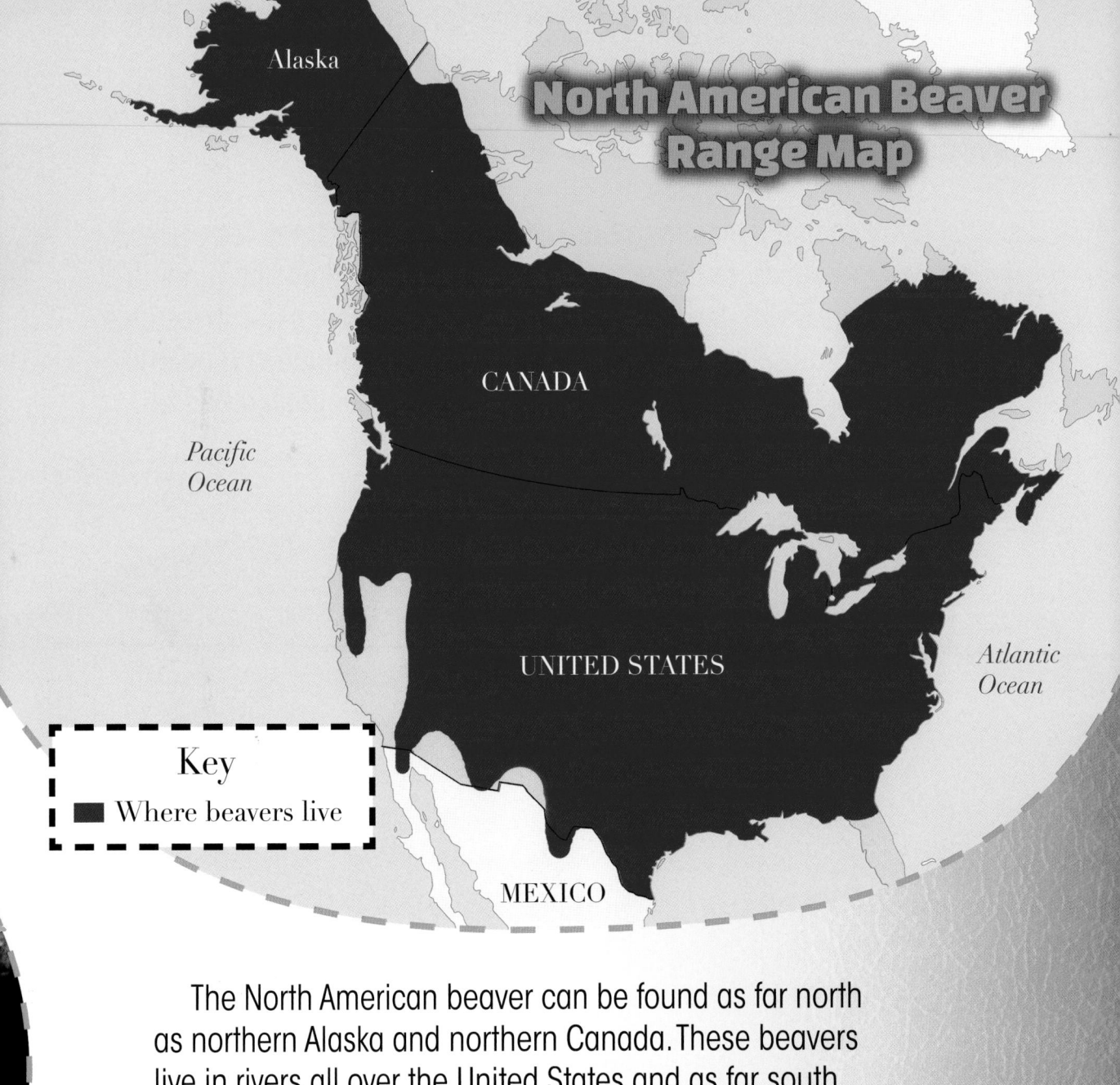

North American Beaver Range Map

Alaska

CANADA

Pacific Ocean

UNITED STATES

Atlantic Ocean

Key

Where beavers live

MEXICO

The North American beaver can be found as far north as northern Alaska and northern Canada. These beavers live in rivers all over the United States and as far south as northern Mexico.

7

Beavers use their strong front teeth to cut down trees. They use the wood to build **dams** across rivers. Behind the dam, the running water slows down and becomes a deep pool. Beavers use this space to build homes, called lodges. Beaver lodges are made of mud and wood. Dams and lodges can be large or small, depending on the size of the river and the size and depth of the pool.

Beaver Lodge

## Beaver Dam

Beavers typically live in **colonies** of between 6 and 12 members. There is usually a pair of parents, their babies, called kits, and sometimes their kits' kits in a single colony.

Beavers usually live for between 10 and 12 years, though some have lived to be nearly 20 years old.

Beavers played an important role in North American culture long before Europeans arrived. In the stories of the Algonquian peoples of the Northeast, beavers helped create land. When Earth was originally covered in water, beavers, otters, and muskrats created land by diving down and bringing up mud.

Beavers were important to many Native American peoples. This traditional outfit, including a beaver hat, was made by the Menominee, who live in what is now Wisconsin.

Native Americans hunted beavers. They made coats and blankets from their fur. Before the arrival of Europeans, Native American tribes killed only as many beavers as they needed to for survival. Once the Dutch, French, and English started paying them to catch more beavers, though, Native Americans started to reduce the population by a lot.

Native Americans often prepared beaver hides by stretching them on a frame made of bent wood like the one here.

**1599**

The French begin building **trading posts** and settlements on the St. Lawrence River in Canada.

**1670**

The Hudson's Bay Company is founded.

1550 1575 1600 1625 1650 1675 1700 1725 1750

**1621**

The Dutch West India Company is founded.

**1701**

The Iroquois, French, and dozens of Native American tribes sign the Great Peace of Montreal, a treaty ending the Beaver Wars.

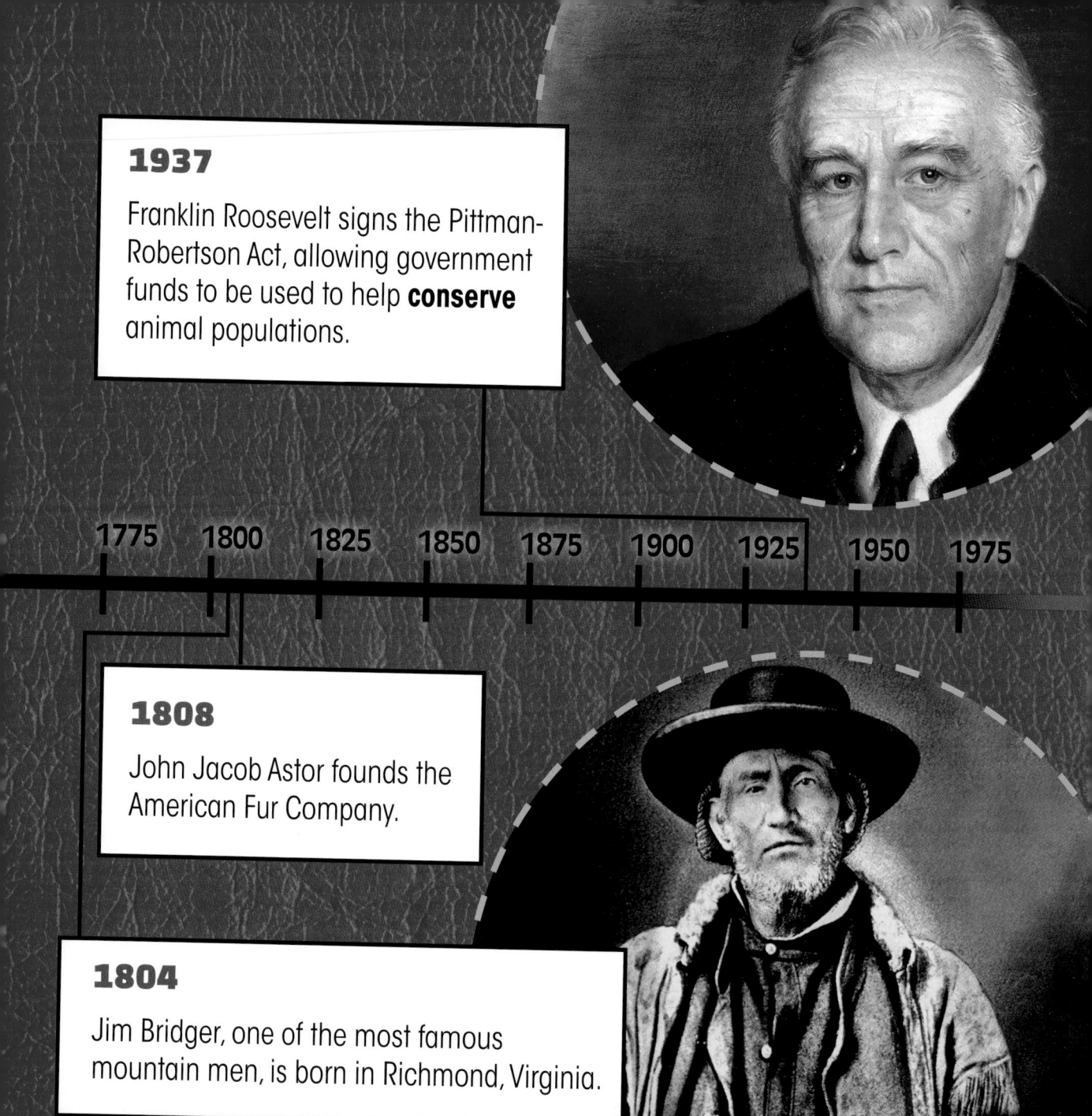

**1937**

Franklin Roosevelt signs the Pittman-Robertson Act, allowing government funds to be used to help **conserve** animal populations.

1775   1800   1825   1850   1875   1900   1925   1950   1975

**1808**

John Jacob Astor founds the American Fur Company.

**1804**

Jim Bridger, one of the most famous mountain men, is born in Richmond, Virginia.

13

# THE FUR TRADE BEGINS

The British, French, and Dutch all came to North America in the early seventeenth century, in part hoping to **profit** from the beaver fur trade. The Dutch made agreements with the Iroquois in modern-day New York State to trade for fur, while the French had trading posts in modern-day Quebec.

There was a big **demand** for beaver furs in Europe. Beautiful bead chains, called wampum, became important in the trade. Certain Native American groups made wampum, which they traded with the Europeans for guns, silver plates, and other metal objects. The Europeans used the wampum to trade for furs with other Native American tribes.

This image shows a group of British merchants trading with the Beothuks, a people who lived in Newfoundland, Canada. The image was first published in Frankfurt, Germany, in 1634.

Before long, the Iroquois had trouble finding enough beaver furs from their own lands to trade with the English and Dutch. They began moving onto lands on which other tribes lived. Some of these tribes were pushed west. Others, already weakened by diseases from Europe, were wiped out. Some tribes that the Iroquois fought with traded furs with the French, who got drawn into the fighting, too.

The Native Americans traded several kinds of beaver pelts, or furs, to the Europeans. The most valued were *castor gras* pelts, which were trapped in winter and worn throughout the trapping season.

The goods that the Europeans traded with Native Americans for furs included guns, cloth, iron tools, glass beads, and metal cooking pots.

Eventually, the Dutch lost their North American colonies to the British. By 1701, the English, French, and 40 Native American tribes had finally made peace. The Iroquois and French now had control over the Great Lakes region.

# MOUNTAIN MEN

Twenty years after winning its freedom in the American Revolution, the United States doubled its size with the Louisiana Purchase. The fur trade drove some of the earliest exploration of these new lands west of the Mississippi River.

Mountain men were men who traveled deep into territory that had not been explored by European Americans. They trapped beavers and other animals. They sold the furs they collected to powerful fur companies at a yearly gathering, called a **rendezvous**.

John Jacob Astor, one of America's first millionaires, founded the American Fur Company. His company gained almost complete control over the American fur business.

These mountain men are setting traps for beavers. The traps were tied to a tree or pole so that a beaver could not swim or walk away with them once it was caught.

Mountain men came from many backgrounds. George Drouillard was part French and part Shawnee. Jim Beckwourth was an African American whose mother was a slave.

# BEAVERS IN DANGER

Over time, trappers killed so many beavers that the animals became rare across the United States. The beaver trade also grew less profitable because beaver hats and other goods made from beaver fur went out of fashion.

Though the beaver fur trade slowed down, Americans' westward expansion continued to hurt the beaver population. In the early twentieth century, conservationists began working to bring back beavers. Almost no beavers had lived in New York's Hudson Valley since the mid-1600s, but conservation efforts helped bring the population back quickly in the 1920s. By the 1950s, their population was back up all over the United States.

Over the last century, people have worked hard to help North America's beaver population return to healthy levels.

21

# BEAVERS TODAY

Trapping beavers is still legal in the United States. The hunting, trapping, and selling of beaver fur is highly **regulated**, though. This means that there are rules about how people can do it.

While beavers have made a comeback in many parts of North America and the world, there are still places where beavers have to deal with **pollution** and **habitat loss**. Luckily, there are many groups that work to keep the beaver population strong and healthy.

Today, scientists think that there are about 10 million beavers in the United States.

**colonies** (KAH-luh-neez) Groups that live together.

**conserve** (kun-SERV) To keep something safe.

**dams** (DAMZ) Large walls built in rivers, which hold water back.

**demand** (dih-MAND) A need or want people have for goods or services.

**economy** (ih-KAH-nuh-mee) The way in which a country or a business oversees its goods and services.

**habitat loss** (HA-buh-tat LAHS) The loss of places in which a plant or animal can naturally live.

**mammals** (MA-mulz) Warm-blooded animals that have backbones and hair, breathe air, and feed milk to their young.

**pollution** (puh-LOO-shun) Man-made wastes that harm Earth's air, land, or water.

**population** (pop-yoo-LAY-shun) A group of animals or people living in the same place.

**profit** (PRAH-fit) To gain or benefit in some way.

**regulated** (REH-gyoo-lay-ted) Controlled something.

**rendezvous** (RON-dih-voo) A French word that means "an agreed-upon place and time to meet."

**trading posts** (TRAYD-ing POHSTS) Places where people come to exchange goods.

# WEBSITES

Due to the changing nature of Internet links, PowerKids Press has developed an online list of websites related to the subject of this book. This site is updated regularly. Please use this link to access the list:

www.powerkidslinks.com/anhi/beav/